SHASTA INDIAN TALES

Retold by
Rosemary Holsinger

Illustrations by
P. I. Piemme

Eagle, Mount Shasta, and Coyote

Naturegraph Publishers, Inc.

Library of Congress Cataloging in Publication Data

Holsinger, Rosemary.
    Shasta Indian tales.

    Bibliography: p.
    1. *Shastan Indians—Legends.*   2. *Indians of North America—California—Legends.*   I. Title.
E99.S332H64   1982   398.2'08997   82-22364

Dedication

To our Siskiyou County Indian friends who delight us with the tales they tell so well — Winnie Nelson (Shasta, Klamath River), Carol Oscar (Karuk, Scott Valley), Madeline Davis (Karuk, Somes Bar, and Sara Nesbitt (Karuk Happy Camp); to the Vinson Brown family of Happy Camp, Perii Hauschild-Owen, and the Siskiyou Arts Council; and to Sharon, Nancy, Su, and Stewart who have tales of their own to tell.

ISBN 978-0-87961-129-3
      0-87961-129-4

Copyright © 1982 Rosemary Holsinger
Funded in part by the Siskiyou Arts Council.
2017 printing

Naturegraph Publishers has been publishing books on natural history, Native Americans, and outdoor subjects since 1946. Free catalog available

Books for a better world

Naturegraph Publishers, Inc.
PO Box 1047 ● 3543 Indian Creek Rd.
Happy Camp, CA 96039
(530) 493-5353
www.naturegraph.com

Table of Contents

LAND OF
THE SHASTAS

Introduction

This is the first in a series of books which relate tales once told by northern California Indian tribes. Subsequent volumes will include selected tales of the Karok, Yurok, Hupa, and others who lived in what is now northernmost California and southern Oregon, most of them on the California side of the border.

We are aware that the Shasta occupied what is now the whole of Siskiyou County, California, and parts of Jackson and Klamath counties in southern Oregon. Imagine a line drawn from Mount Shasta, through Butte Valley to Mount Pitt, then west to where Bear Creek and the Rogue River join, southwest along the divide between Bear Creek and Applegate Creek, west along the ridge of the Siskiyou Mountains and the drainage area of the Klamath River nearly to the present site of Happy Camp, then south and east along the edge of Scott River and the Shasta Dam drainage areas to Mount Shasta—and you will have drawn the boundaries of the Shasta dwellings and activities, a vast area indeed.

The Shasta were a peace-loving people. A headman at each village site led them to live in peace, to do good, have kind hearts, and to be industrious. They took no more from nature than they needed for subsistence. Their food included meat of deer, bear, fowl, small mammals, salmon, trout, eel, turtles, mussels, grasshoppers, and crickets. They gathered and ate acorns, nuts, seeds, bulbs, roots, greens, and berries. They had milkweed as a chewing gum, and they prepared a delicious drink from manzanita berries.

They made their own utensils. From wood they created pipes, mush paddles, digging sticks, and spoons. From bone or horn of deer they fashioned scrapers, wedges, awls, arrow-flakers, pestles, and knives.

For fun, the Shasta ran races or played games. During the waning of the moon in December and January each year, adults played a ring and pin game related to the tale they told concerning ten moons, five of which were killed to make the winter shorter. (See *Coyote and the Ten Moons*, p. 16) And they played musical instruments: hide drums, bone flutes, and deer hoof rattles.

Storytelling was mainly done for the children, though adults would sometimes use stories to illustrate points they wished to make. At the end of the story, the teller of the tale (usually an older woman, perhaps a grandmother) would take each of the children in turn and, pressing on the child's vertebrae starting in the neck, would name different animal characteristics the child should have, such as "You must be sharp-eyed and brave as the eagle." And so the child would try to be.

Many Shasta tales feature the character Coyote. He will be both greedy and a hero, doing mischievous things as well as good ones. Sometimes he finds himself in real trouble.

So now, enjoy the tales.

Rosemary Holsinger
P. I. Piemme
Yreka, California
October, 1982

MOUNT SHASTA TALES

Great Spirit Makes the Mountain

In far northern California the Indians speak of Mount Shasta. "It was made before any other mountain in the world," they will say.

Great Spirit saw below him that all the land was flat. He thought to make a mountain so high that it could be seen by everyone. He made a hole through the sky. Then he pushed ice and snow down and down, and then he pushed some more down. It made a mound on the flat land below. It grew larger. It grew higher until it became the highest mountain in the land. It was so high that its top pushed its way up through the clouds.

Great Spirit stepped down out of the clouds onto his great snowy mountain. Then he stepped down onto the land and looked at his beautiful mountain.

"I will call you Shasta because you are white and pure," he said. "Trees, grow!" he said, and many beautiful green pine trees and cedar trees grew fast and tall.

"Sun, melt some snow so the trees may drink and remain green!" he said. And Sun did as he was asked, and the water came so fast that rivers and creeks ran full.

"The trees need birds to live in their branches," said Great Spirit as he picked some leaves from the trees.

He blew on the leaves and they became birds.

Then Great Spirit felt the birds should have companions. From a tree he took a stick and broke it into many pieces. The small pieces he threw gently into the streams and said, "You are fishes to swim in the streams."

The middle-size pieces he threw into the forest, "You will become the smaller animals."

The largest pieces he threw about him, "You shall become the largest animal in the forest and shall be called Grizzly Bear."

Later, Great Spirit worried about creating Grizzly Bear because that large animal became ferocious.

All became a part of the great mountain.

And that is how it was in the beginning.

The Maiden Who Perished in the Snow

A great Indian Chief who lived at the foot of the great white mountain had a very beautiful daughter who refused all suitors.

Wyeka,* the Indian God, dwelt in his shelter on the very peak of Mount Shasta. This God of the mountain was a good God, the God of Purity. One day, Wyeka saw the beautiful Indian maiden and loved her. He carried her to his home on the mountain top, but there the pretty Indian maiden died of grief. The God, in his sadness, decreed that the mountain would always be covered with snow to signify the Indian maiden's purity. The Indians believed that the God Wyeka carried her away to her death, but he intended only to have her share eternity with him.

The Legend of Thumb Rock

More than halfway up Mount Shasta stands Thumb Rock, an immense precipice that protrudes from the rest of the slope. Many years ago, before gold was discovered at Yreka, Siskiyou County was inhabited by the first Americans, the Indians.

At the foot of the mountain where the town of Mount Shasta City is now located, a great Chief lived with his tribe. This tribe was the most peaceful one around, and the Chief liked to have members of the other tribes visit him.

This Chief, too, had a very beautiful daughter, sought by many fine young warriors. Among the Indian tribes then, a girl could not choose her husband but was sold for a certain amount of money, the amount depending on her social standing. Thus it was with the Chief's daughter.

Chief Big Rock of the Modoc tribe had given her father payment for her. The next day he was to take the Chief's daughter home as his squaw. But she was in love with Flying Eagle, the handsome son of the medicine man. She opposed her father when he told her of her future husband.

The young Indian maiden found Flying Eagle and told him of

---

*Wyeka (or Ieka) is the Shastan-speaking Indian peoples' word for "Great White," or purity; "Great White" is what they called Mount Shasta.

her plight. They ran away together that night. By morning, they knew they would be far away from Chief Big Rock.

They started out toward the East where they thought they would find some camp for the night and safety with another tribe. Far into the night they went, but they found no one.

"Flying Eagle," she whispered, "where are we? It seems to me we are climbing a slope."

"Yes," he answered, "but perhaps it's just a hill. It is so foggy I cannot see, but let's keep on going."

They went on and on until the trees began to get scarce. Now there was frozen snow under their feet. They did not know the danger they were in, that they were climbing Mount Shasta. If they stopped for a moment to rest, the cold was so intense it would freeze their blood. Finally, the maiden could go no farther. They stopped in the shelter of a huge rock and sat down to rest.

Days later an Indian guide sent by Chief Big Rock found them, frozen. The guide said that both of the maiden's thumbs were pointing outward and the rock they were under was in the shape of a thumb pointing the same way as the maiden's.

This story was told afterwards as a warning to Indians never to attempt to climb the mountain. To this day no Indian in this vicinity will consent to climb Mount Shasta.

Coyote and the Flood

Coyote was walking by the water carrying his bow and arrows. There was an evil one in the water who caused the water to rise up toward Coyote. It washed over him. Coyote was covered by the water. Then the water went down. Coyote saw the evil one rise up. Coyote shot him with an arrow.

Coyote then ran away, but the water followed after him. Coyote ran and ran, and still the water rose higher and higher.

Coyote ran to the top of Mount Shasta and the water rose higher and higher until all the animals were swimming about. Grizzly Bear and Black Bear swam for their lives, Deer swam and Elk, Wild-Cat, Wolf, and Mountain Lion swam this way and that. And the little animals swam and swam, fearing for their lives— Gray Squirrel and Ground Squirrel, Jack Rabbit, Badger, Porcupine, and Raccoon. All the animals swam and swam.

9

Coyote ran up on Mount Shasta and still the water rose until there was only a little piece of ground showing above it at the very top of the mountain. There was just enough ground to build a fire on.

Then the water went down...it went down...it went down...and down...and down. And it was swampy everywhere.

The animals scattered all about and found their homes again.

Coyote and his people watch the flood waters rise.

Eagle and Wind's Daughters

On the top of Mount Shasta lived Great Wind. She had two daughters and many people came hoping to buy them as wives. Every time anyone tried to reach the place where the girls lived, they could not, for Great Wind blew them back. So many had been blown back that people were scattered about everywhere. The old woman did not want her daughters to marry.

Eagle had been watching what Great Wind did.

"Now I must try!" he said. "I wonder if I can get there?" So he went.

Eagle liked to sing, so he sang as he went along. Coyote, on the ground below setting snares for gophers, said to himself, "Where is it that someone is coming?" He listened and thought, "It sounds like a song. It *is* a song!" He kept listening.

The sound came nearer. Coyote looked all about.

"Where is it that someone is singing?" he said.

Then Eagle came, flying.

"Eagle! Where are you going?"

But Eagle only went on singing all the time.

"I want to go, too!" said Coyote. "Wait for me, Eagle!"

"Well, you can come, too," said Eagle. So they went on together.

Eagle put Coyote inside his shirt, and they went on this way, went to buy wives, singing as they went.

Soon the Great Wind roared nearby. She blew and blew. As they got to the bottom of the hill, she blew Coyote out. Great Wind tore open Eagle's shirt and blew out what he carried there. But Eagle kept on. Great Wind blew very hard. The skirt of hail that old Great Wind wore rattled as she turned round. Eagle was blown far back.

Great Wind blows Eagle and Coyote away.

11

Again, Eagle came on and got nearer. Then he got very close, got over the smoke-hole, and then he went in through it. Again he was blown back many times. Finally, he darted in suddenly as there came a lull in the wind. He sat down. Great Wind lifted him off the ground where he sat, but the old woman could do nothing more with him. Great Wind blew the great logs in the fire all about, but Eagle still sat there. Finally, Great Wind gave up.

Eagle was the only one who ever got there to buy wives.

Coyote and the Yellow Jackets

There was a fish weir* on the river and many people were drying salmon. Coyote was living upriver and thought he would also go and get some salmon. So he went to the fish weir and the people gave him a great amount of salmon.** He tried to lift the load, but it was so heavy he had to put it down once to get a better hold. Then he heaved it up on his back, and went off.

After awhile he thought he would rest.—"I will take a nap as there is all day to rest."

So Coyote went to sleep, using the pack of salmon as his pillow. When he awoke he was hungry. It was still early in the day, so he reached for his pack of salmon and took a bite. But it was pine bark he bit into, for while he was sleeping some Yellow Jackets had come and taken his salmon, leaving pine bark in its place. Coyote was furious.

"Who did this?" he yelled. But he saw no tracks, so he went back to the fish weir where the people were. He told them what had happened. They offered him more salmon.

The next day Coyote started off again with his new pack of salmon and stopped to rest in the same place. This time he pretended to sleep for he wanted to see who had taken his salmon before. Soon the Yellow Jackets came and lit on his pack of salmon. There were so many Yellow Jackets that they were able to lift the pack and fly away with it. Coyote tried to follow them but soon tired.

---

*Weir—a frame of rods or twigs braided together as an enclosure in a stream to catch fish.

**It is a customary courtesy to give visitors and travelers what they ask for.

Then he went back and told the people at the fish weir that it was Yellow Jackets and of how they had again taken his salmon. The people became curious, but gave him more salmon and went with him to the same spot where he had stopped to rest twice before. They all sat and waited and watched, for the people also wanted to see the Yellow Jackets take the salmon away.

But while they waited, Turtle came along.

Coyote asked Turtle, "Who told you to come?"

Turtle said nothing but sat apart from the others and waited.

Now, finally, the Yellow Jackets came. They lifted the load of salmon up and then put it down again as it was very heavy. Then they managed to lift it with all their strength and flew away with it as they had done before. The people followed them. The Yellow Jackets flew in a straight line to where Mount Shasta stands. The people followed them up the valley and the river, to Mount Shasta.

Coyote got tired and had to stop to rest. Then, one by one, the people, too, got tired and dropped out scattered along the way, leaving only Turtle to continue; but, Turtle still went on following the Yellow Jackets who kept flying with the salmon.

They flew up the mountain with Turtle after them. Then, at the very top of Mount Shasta, the Yellow Jackets flew in a hole, still carrying the salmon.

Coyote saw Turtle and his great accomplishment and thought sadly, "I was the first to drop out, and there is Turtle still following!"

Now all the people, having rested, came up to the mountain top. They tried to smoke the Yellow Jackets out, and the smoke came up far away in a place in the valley. Coyote ran very fast wanting to stop up the hole, but the smoke just came out again in another place. So again Coyote ran fast and stopped it up. The people helped too, fanning the smoke into the house of the Yellow Jackets. But the smoke kept coming up here and there and soon it was rising out of many places in the mountain.

So the people gave up. They could not smoke the Yellow Jackets out. Nor could they stop the many smokes that rose from the mountain and the valley.* Then the people scattered all about. That is what the story said long ago.

---

*Shasta Valley at the foot of Mount Shasta is covered with small volcanic vents. This tale likely arose to explain the occasional smoke which rises at various locations on the mountain and in the valley near its base.

ORIGINS

How People Came To Be

Some say Eagle made people. When all the water was gone, he sent down his two children, a boy and a girl. That was the beginning.

"Our father sent us to this place to people the earth," the young man said.

"Very well," said the girl.

So they created children and many people came to be, for no one died. Then a boy died and Coyote said, "Maybe it is good, for people will be sad and cry."

And so they buried the boy and death came to be known.

The eagle made people.

Why Cricket Is Black

In the beginning many people came to be. Then one died. It was Cricket's child.

"What shall we do?" they cried.

All gathered together.

Some said, "Let us have people come to life again. Let us not bury them!"

"Stop!" said others. "Let us go and tell Coyote. He does not know this has happened."

Coyote came.

"What do you think?" they asked him. "We were saying that the dead should come back again."

"Why do you say that?" Coyote said. "Bury him. He is dead. If people come back, the world will be too full. Around this world is water. The world will be so full we will all be pushed into the water." So they buried Cricket's child and cried.

Five days after this they finished the sweating.* They felt sad. They thought, "If only Coyote's child would die." Coyote's child did die and Coyote cried.

"My child is dead. Let us have people come back to life."

"No!" they said.

"If he should come back to life, my child that died would not smell good. He has decayed," said Cricket.

They all agreed.

"Coyote, you said that the dead would otherwise fill up the world."

Cricket pitched himself all black to show his mourning. He mourned forever.

Coyote soon buried his son and cried.

That is the way the first people died.

That was the first death.

*Sweating in the sweat lodge was practiced for days following the death of a husband, wife, or child. When Black Cricket's child died, as noted here, Coyote said it should not be brought back to life. Mourners made themselves black, like Cricket, with pitch.

Coyote and the Ten Moons

Long ago when the first people came there were ten Moons.* The people talked together.

"Shall we kill the ten Moons?" they said. "The winters are too long."

"Yes," said Coyote, who was there with them. "I can kill them. I will do it."

The Moons lived far to the east with a great bird called Toruk. The Moons had taken out his leg bones so he could not get away. Every day they went to gather roots and left Toruk to guard their house. He cried when he was left alone. When he got hungry he would cry a hungry cry and one of the Moons would come and feed him.

Every night the Moons brought back roots. Once one came bringing big snowflakes with him. One came with a shower of rain. Another brought large hailstones. And one brought strong winds so that huge trees were blown over.

The people told Coyote, "Yes, go, kill the Moons."

"I will fool them well," said Coyote.

So Coyote went to kill the Moons. When he arrived where they lived, he found they were gone gathering roots, and Toruk was there alone. Toruk was frightened to see Coyote and almost called out a warning to the Moons.

But Coyote said, "Be still. I am a friend. Here is food for you. Eat it. I will fix your legs." And Coyote cut up oak and made wooden legs for Toruk.

"What do the Moons do for you?" Coyote asked.

"They bring me food when I am hungry. I cry and one of them brings me food," said Toruk.

"Good!" said Coyote. "Cry now and a Moon will come."

So Toruk cried out, "Oo-oo-oo!"

Far away, the Moons heard Toruk's cry.

"Ha!" said they, "Toruk is hungry. You," and they pointed to one, "take him food."

"All right," said the one, and he went.

"One is coming!" Toruk said.

Then Storm Moon came and poured much rain.

---

*To the Indians, a moon referred to a month of time. Thus, ten moons meant ten months. At that time all ten were winter months.

Coyote hid behind the door and watched for Storm Moon to come in. Soon Storm Moon came and when he put his head in the door Coyote seized him by the hair and cut off his head. Then he threw the head behind the door and his body to the other side of the house.

Coyote warmed his hands by the fire until he felt warm again.

"Now, cry again, Toruk!" said Coyote.

"Very well," said Toruk, "Oo-oo-oo!"

"Ha! That bird is not satisfied," said the Moons, hearing his cry. "You go this time," they said, pointing to one.

"All right," said Snowflake Moon, and he went.

"One is coming!" Toruk said.

Then Snowflake Moon came, scattering snow.

Coyote hid behind the door and watched for Snowflake Moon to come in. Soon he did, and when he put his head in the door Coyote seized him by the hair and cut off his head. Then he threw the head behind the door and his body to the other side of the house.

Coyote warmed his hands by the fire until he felt warm again.

"Now, Toruk, cry again!" said Coyote.

"Very well," said Toruk, "Oo-oo-oo!"

"Ha! That bird is not satisfied," said the Moons, hearing his cry. "You go this time," they said, pointing to one.

"All right," said Wind Moon.

So Wind Moon came to the house, blowing wind and pouring rain. As he came in, Coyote seized him by the hair and cut off his head. The head was thrown behind the door, the body to the other side of the house.

Coyote, all wet from the rain and blown about by the wind the Moon had brought, warmed his hands by the fire and tried to dry himself.

"Cry again!" he said to Toruk.

"Oo-oo-oo!" cried Toruk.

"Ah! What is the matter with that bird?" said the Moons. "He is crying again. You better go," they said to Hailstone Moon.

"All right," he said.

"Here comes the Hailstone Moon!" Toruk said.

Coyote felt chilled from the cold that Hailstone Moon brought, but taking a deep breath, he was able to seize Hailstone

Moon by the hair. Though hailstones hit him hard, falling to the floor and nearly making him fall, Coyote managed to cut off Hailstone Moon's head. The head went behind the door; the body across to the other side of the house.

"Oo-oo-oo!" Toruk cried for the fourth time. And there came Tornado Moon, blowing down trees in his way and nearly blowing away the Moons' own house. It was hard for Coyote to get hold of Tornado Moon's hair, but he did, and soon Tornado Moon's head was rolling on the floor. But instead of rolling behind the door it rolled to the fireplace where the hair began to burn. It smelled bad.

Toruk heard the Biggest Moon coming.

"Biggest Moon is coming!" Toruk cried. "He smelled Tornado Moon's hair burning!"

By this time Coyote was so cold he was nearly frozen stiff. He was numb. He warmed himself by the fire, stomping out the burning hair. Now Coyote was ready for the Biggest-Moon-of-All.

"Let us run away after this one," Toruk said. "The other Moons are not so strong and will live here quietly and not bother the people."

Coyote battles Hailstone Moon while Toruk looks on.

18

"We will do that," said Coyote as Biggest-Moon-of-All stumbled through the door. As he rose to beat Coyote, Coyote cut off his head with two blows. Then Coyote and Toruk ran and got away.

Had Coyote not done this killing, there would have been ten moons. Coyote killed five of them, so winter does not last all year.

Why the Sun Rolls Along

Sun was warned by a messenger, "Someone is coming to kill you."

Soon a person came along and seized the sun. He threw him toward the East, but Sun came back. He threw him toward the South, but Sun came back. The evil one came toward Sun again, but Sun began to roll along. Sun rolled and rolled and rolled along. He rolls along to this very day.

How Strawberry Valley Got Its Name

Many, many years ago at the edge of the valley known as Strawberry Valley* lived a tribe of Indians. The daughter of the Chief was very beautiful. At the other end of the valley lived another tribe of Indians. A young warrior lived there.

One day as the young Indian princess was out walking, she met the young warrior. Although the two tribes were enemies, the maiden and warrior forgot this as they looked into each other's eyes.

The next day she came again, seeking him but she did not see him. She returned many times. One day, as she was seated on a pile of straw, she saw him. He came nearer to her, and they sat and talked for a long time.

Meanwhile, her father the Chief had missed her. He went in search of her and finally saw the two seated together on the pile

*Today Strawberry Valley is located by the town of Mount Shasta City in northern California.

of straw. He knew the warrior at once as the son of the enemy Chief. He was very angry and called on the God of the Mountain to punish his daughter and her friend. The God asked her to return home and remain with her father. She refused to do this, and so she was punished.

"You shall always creep along the ground," she was told. "Each year when your berries come out, people shall call them *strawberries*. Your children will continually try to escape from you along your vines as you have done from your father."

And that is what happened. And that is how Strawberry Valley got its name.

Why the Stars Are Scattered in the Sky

Long, long ago, they say, when all began to move upon the land again after the great flood, people were as brothers though they lived far apart. Some moved south, and a little Indian girl was left behind. A voice called, "Little Girl, come here." The little girl followed the voice to a place near a running stream where she stumbled over a little bag made of white, hand-woven cotton.

"Carry this on your back," the voice said. "Do not unwrap what is in the bag."

The little girl promised not to uncover it. But as she went along she began to wonder why she should not open the bag a little and see what was in it.

She stopped. She put her bundle on the ground and bent over it, untying many difficult knots. She came to the last knot. The bag was overflowing with something and she wanted more and more to know what it was.

As something began to burst out, she tried to stop it and to quickly tie the knots again; but, it was too late. The bag emptied, and its contents flew out into the sky and scattered all over the heavens as bright stars.

Once, all the stars were to have been given names and placed in special places, but now they were scattered and it would be many, many moons before they could be given the names they now bear.*

*This story may bring to mind the story of Pandora and the box—curiosity got the better of both maidens! A variant ending to this tale would have the little girl capture a few of the stars and quickly tie the knots again on the bag. Then, when she came to the end of her journey, she would unwrap the few stars remaining and put them in their right places. The story would conclude, "We know only a few stars by name: The Slingshot Stars, the Pot-Rest Stars, the Shield Stars (Big Dipper), and a few others."

ACTIVITIES

Coyote Gambles

Coyote lived by the river. He had a wife and ten children—five boys and five girls. He gambled all the time. He lost all the time. He lost all his things gambling. He lost his beads gambling. He lost his house gambling.

One day he had nothing left to bet. So he thought he would bet his youngest child. So he did. Then he bet another child, and another, and another, until all ten children were gone. Coyote lost them all. His wife sat very still. He saw her.

"Now I bet you," he said.

He lost. He lost his wife. He lost his beads, his house, he lost ten children and his wife!

"I will stop playing," he thought.

He went away from his river home. He went far away. He went to a valley. He became thin as he had nothing to eat. He saw grasshoppers. He caught and ate some. They were sweet. But he did not find enough food, and no meat. He was all bones. He saw a fire burning and went to it but got too close to it and it burned his hair. He ran to a creek but it was dried up.

Far away was a big river. He ran to it but he soon was burned all up except his head.* He reached the water and jumped in. Then he went back to the place where he had lived before. He went back to the place where he had gambled. That is all.

The Wrestling Match

Kaletsa the bird lived with his nine brothers. There were ten brothers altogether. Now, one went off to hunt for deer and did

---

*One must never worry about Coyote. Even though he "dies" or "eats himself up," he will appear in another tale across the Indian nations. He sometimes seems to be a magical person. If he is unable to help himself, the birds or Fox will help him.

not return. A second one went and did not return. A third went, and still another and another until all had gone except Kaletsa, the tenth and youngest. The youngest went.

He saw a big man and thought, "That one has all the time been killing my brothers."

"Let us wrestle!" said the big man.

"I am so small!" said Kaletsa. The big man was called Giant.

"Let us wrestle!" he repeated.

"No, I will not wrestle. You are too big," said little Kaletsa. Then he changed his mind. "Well! I'll wrestle after all."

So they wrestled.

Now Kaletsa saw some water. He thought, "Giant threw my brothers in the water."

So Kaletsa, youngest of the brothers, lifted Giant. And then he threw him into the river, and so he killed him. Then he went to the river. He picked up the bones of his brothers and went home. He took them inside the lodge, took them into the sweat lodge, made a fire and, placing the bones inside the sweat lodge, he himself went and lay outside.

Then he heard something, heard lots of people talking inside the sweat lodge. By and by they said, "Open the door!" So he opened it. Then they came out, nine of them came out alive again. His brothers lived again.

Coyote and Beaver

Coyote was traveling along a trail one day when he met someone coming towards him. It was Beaver.

"Where are you going?" Coyote asked. Beaver did not answer.

"Didn't you hear me?" shouted Coyote. But Beaver went on.

"I did not kill your child," said Coyote. "Your child died because he ate wood."

They each went on their way. Soon Coyote sat down and along came Beaver behind him. Beaver wanted to catch Coyote and kill him.

Coyote ran, for he was afraid of Beaver. But soon he got tired and stopped again. Beaver came on.

"Where are you going?" Coyote asked.

Beaver did not answer but seized Coyote.

There was no water around, so Beaver said, "Let a lake come to me!"

Coyote was frightened.

"Let go of me!" he cried, and said—"Let the lake *not* come! Let go of me!"

The water came and grew deeper. It covered over Coyote and he died. Then the water went away. That is all.

Beaver remains silent.

Winning Gambling Luck

At Seiad* long ago people lived. They liked to gamble all the time. Many more people came and gambled. From one man they won all he had.

After awhile he even bet his wife, so they won her, too. Now he had nothing at all and he didn't know what to do. He went off.

"I wonder what I will do," he thought.

He went up into the mountains.

He thought, "I wish to go to that place."

That place was where there was a lake. He went there. He jumped into it. In the lake was a great rattlesnake. It swallowed him, like that.

Now at his home they worried about him. They missed him.

---

*Seiad is a small town in northern California east of Happy Camp on the Klamath River.

They did not know where he had gone. All hunted him. Even his brother hunted him.

After five days the snake spit out the man he had swallowed. On the sixth day his brother found him lying on the ground.

"Perhaps he is dead," thought the brother. He touched him and saw that he breathed. He raised him up. He dragged him higher up on shore and washed him clean. Then he took him home. Now he gambled again but now he won back as much as he had lost.

That was the way he got his gambling luck.

Winning gambling luck.

Coyote and the Pitch Stump

Coyote was walking along when he saw Pitch Stump.
"Where are you going?" asked Coyote.
But Pitch did not answer. He really was not going anywhere.
Coyote was angry and walked up to him.
"What is the matter with you? Didn't you hear me?"
Pitch still did not answer.
Coyote grabbed him and Pitch held him. Coyote was stuck.
"Let me go or I'll kick you!" Coyote was really angry now. He

kicked Pitch, and Pitch now held him tight. Coyote was wobbling on his one free foot.

"Let me go or I'll kill you with my other foot!" he screamed. He kicked with his other foot. This, too, stuck fast, for Pitch holds all. Coyote was in an embarrassing position.

"I can kill anything, you evil one, with my tail!" And Coyote hit Pitch with his tail. Pitch held that, too.

"I will bite you with my mouth!" Coyote was now on his last defense. His mouth stuck, too, and he could hardly breathe.

"Oh, my Aunt," Coyote said, "set fire to Pitch."

Coyote suddenly was free, for fire burned hot on Pitch and he had to release his hold on Coyote.

"You will remain nothing but pitch," Coyote said.

To this day Pitch remains sticky and feeds a fire well.

"I will bite you with my mouth!"

Racing With Thunder

Thunder and Silver Fox lived near each other. They liked to bet with each other.

26

"Let's run a race," said Silver Fox.

"All right!" said Thunder.

So they ran a race. Thunder won over Silver Fox. And he won over Red Fox, and then he won over Black Fox. There were ten brother foxes all together. They talked together and said, "We must ask Wolf to help us."

And so they did.

"What can I do?" asked Wolf.

"Come, we will hide you. This is what Thunder does to us. He nearly kills us. He tears up the ground as he runs in front of us."

Day came and Thunder raced again. He tore up the ground. He tore open trees and made the earth rough for Wolf to run over. Wolf kept praying for help. Suddenly Wolf pulled a Pain from his tongue and threw it to the ground in front of Thunder. When Thunder stepped on Pain, he stopped still. Wolf ran on and won the race. Wolf was the only one who could run faster than Thunder.

That is how the brothers Fox won over Thunder.

Coyote and His Grandmother

Coyote and his grandmother lived together but did not always get along. The grandmother thought Coyote did not tell her the truth, though he *usually* did.

It was winter and he said, "I will go hunt deer."

"Very well," she said. "Go hunt deer."

So Coyote went to hunt fawn tracks, but in winter there are no fawn tracks because fawns are usually born in the spring of the year. So he went home and said, "There are no fawns."

"I do not believe what you tell me," the grandmother scolded. "You must not say there are no fawn tracks."

Coyote merely said, "There are no fawn tracks about. I will go now and throw all the dog-salmon* in the river."

"Why do that?" his grandmother asked.

"It will not keep," said Coyote.

"You must not say that," the grandmother said. "We will be hungry this winter."

---

*Dog-salmon is not the best salmon one can eat.

27

Coyote threw the dog-salmon in the river anyway. He was tired of eating it.

They became hungry. His grandmother cried, though she had hidden some salmon meat under her pillow.

It snowed and snowed. In the morning Coyote could not open the door to go out. He pushed and pushed but it would not open. The snow outside held the door shut.

They were both in the house, hungry. The grandmother lay on the side next to the wall. Coyote lay behind the fire and was starving. He heard funny sounds and looked up. He thought that his grandmother was eating her deerskin blanket. It was his grandmother all right, but she was nibbling on the salmon meat she had hidden under her pillow. He went to her and jerked her blanket off. Coyote was angry.

"Why do you eat and give me none?" he shouted. She cried.

The next day they were still hungry as the salmon was gone.

"What can we eat?" he shouted. "I know, I will eat myself all up." So Coyote ate himself all up, all except his tail. He ate his deerskin blanket, and both Coyote and his grandmother kept on doing this until spring came and thawed the snow.

Coyote and the Grizzly Bears

Many people lived and Coyote lived among them. One day Coyote said, "Let us go and drive game with fire."

"Very well," they said. So they went.

Coyote went on ahead and fixed an arrow-point securely by wrapping it to the shaft. Grizzly Bear came along and picked up Coyote's arrow. Coyote took it and hit his hand with it.

"That is not an arrow-point," Grizzly Bear said. "You cannot shoot with that." The people looked at Grizzly Bear. He was acting strange.

They sat down. Lizard pulled an arrow out of his quiver. The arrow-point was stuck on with pitch.

"Give it to me," said Grizzly Bear.

He stuck his hand with the arrow-point. Then he threw away the arrow. They looked at him. Grizzly Bear waved his hand.

"I guess that is blood!" he said.

Lizard saw that something was wrong.

"Now let us all go and hunt," he said.

All went off except Coyote. He hid and watched Grizzly Bear. The bear seemed to be very sick. He was not himself. He dug at the ground, he grew angry, he ran at the trees and bit them. Then he sat down. He waved his hands about and lay on his back.

"M-m-m," he said and he died.

Coyote ran up to him and saw that he had died.

"Grizzly Bear is dead," he called out.

All the people out driving deer with fire came back and gathered around where Grizzly Bear lay.

"Let us burn the fur off," they said. They turned to Lizard.

"Tell us quickly what to do!" said Coyote.

"Skin him without cutting the skin," said Lizard.

Coyote started butchering Grizzly Bear. He left the claws on the hide. He left the teeth.

"Which of you will taste it first?" said Coyote.

"I want to taste first," said the Jay. He did so, then fell over, dead.

The bear seemed to be very sick. He was not himself.

Next, Coyote divided the meat equally all around, and they went away. In the evening, he dressed the hide. Next day he danced.

"Who will be the first to run up and down the line?" said Coyote.

"I will be first," said Tsidi, a small yellow bird.

The people were dancing and Tsidi became afraid. He hid. Then Lizard put on the bearskin and jumped in front of the dancers. They looked at him.

Tsidi felt stronger. "I'll put on the bearskin," he said. He went in front of the dancers and flew up in the air.

"That is good," everybody said.

Next day the Grizzly Bears came.

"Your brother has gone back," said Coyote. "There are his tracks." He pointed at the ground.

But the eleven Grizzly Bears could not find them. In the evening the people said, "Let us dance!"

So they danced.

The Grizzly Bears sat there watching them.

"Let us jump in front of the dancers," said all the bears.

Then Lizard jumped out in front of the Grizzly Bears with the bearskin on.

The Grizzly Bears cried. All stopped dancing and went to sleep.

But the Grizzly Bears were angry. They ran about outside the house, dodging this way and that. The people did not have weapons to kill them with. Only Lizard did.

"Tomorrow I think we will fight with arrows," said the Grizzly Bears.

Next day they fought. They killed Coyote first. They bit him to pieces. But many of them were killed, too, and blood was everywhere. In the evening all stopped fighting. Then the Grizzly Bears went away, going in all directions. Six had been killed. Only five were left. Coyote was killed for good. Then Lizard and all the others went home to their own places. That is one story.

Coyote Steals Fire

In the beginning, a long time ago, people had only stones for fire. It had started with only one fire-stone, and Pain had that.

"Where Pain lives, there is fire," it was said.

Coyote heard this and decided to steal the fire-stone. He went to Pain's house but only Pain's children were there. The children had been told to beware of Coyote.

"If anyone comes, it will be Coyote," the parents had told them.

When Coyote entered Pain's house, the children said, "We think you are Coyote."

"Why, no," said Coyote, pointing a great distance away—"That is Coyote country."

Coyote stretched his feet out, warming himself by the fire-stone.

"You smell like Coyote," said the children.

Coyote's blanket began to burn and he was ready to run to spread the fire. He called to Chicken-Hawk.

"You smell like Coyote."

"You stand there. I will run with the fire. I will give it to you and then you run on. Eagle! Stand there! Grouse! Stand there! Quail! Stand there!"

Only Turtle did not know about the stolen fire as he was walking beside the river.

So Coyote stole Pain's fire. He ran with it, first giving it to Chicken-Hawk, who ran with it and gave it to Eagle. Eagle flew on and gave it to Grouse, who ran on and gave it to Quail. Quail, not having been told what to do with it but run on, came upon Turtle by the river.

"Here, take it!"

Turtle put the fire under his armpit and jumped into the river, diving deep.*

All the little Pains stood on the riverbank watching.

Coyote soon came up and asked, "Where is the fire?"

"Turtle dove with it," they said.

Coyote was very angry.

Turtle soon crawled out on the other side of the river.

"Where is the fire?" Coyote called.

Turtle, having kept the fire going in his armpit, said, "You keep quiet. I will throw the fire all about so everyone can have it."

And everyone, except Coyote, was glad for now they each had fire.

---

*Only in such a magical tale as this would the fire not burn Turtle's skin or the water not put out the fire.

32

THE LOST ONES

The Lost Brother

Two brothers lived together, Erikaner and Adihotiki.
"Drive the deer toward me," said Erikaner to his brother one day in the woods. Adihotiki did as he was told though he became startled to see a doe lying dead at his brother's feet.
"Why does a doe lie here?" he asked. "What I drove toward you had antlers!"
Unknown to Adihotiki, each time Erikaner had shot the buck he had broken off pieces of the antlers. This happened several times before Adihotiki discovered Erikaner's trick.
Screech Owl was hungry for meat and knew the two brothers had some. Owl turned himself into a little dog and began eating the deer meat until he grew bigger and bigger, and then he carried Adihotiki off.
Erikaner heard his brother scream and came running out of the house. He went to Spider, realizing she would know where his brother was taken.
"He is over on the other side of the river," said Spider. "Badger watched him. Take this little mouse, this little snake, and these cattails. The people will sleep when you sprinkle this last on them. You will have to kill Badger."
Erikaner soon reached the river and saw Badger splitting pitch wood. He picked up a big stone and killed Badger. Then he skinned him and wore his skin. He got to the other side of the river where his brother was being held. Adihotiki recognized him.
That night, Erikaner took out the little snake and the little mouse, sat by the door and watched while the snake caused lightning by its tongue and the mouse spread cattail pollen down over all. The people slept soundly. Then Erikaner went to his brother and cut him down and set fire to the house. All burned as the two brothers escaped.
They continued to follow and kill deer as they needed the meat or the skin.
"People will follow deer as we have," said Erikaner. "They shall run far around, they shall not get out of breath, they shall have long wind."
And so it has been.

Screech owl carries Adihotiki off.

The Captive of the Little Men

Long ago there were many Indians living at Seiad. A man went out to hunt and the Little Men took him prisoner while he was hunting in the mountains.

They took him to their house which seemed to be full of dried deer meat, berries, and other things packed in baskets along the wall. They gave him meat and berries to eat.

At his home, his people worried about him.

"The man is lost. We must hunt for him."

Many went to hunt for him, but they could not find him anywhere.

His wife cried. "Where is he now?" She was crying herself to death. His children cried, too.

All the time he was a prisoner of the Little Men.
Everyone gave up trying to find him.
"Where can anyone find him?" So they gave up.
He had been lost in summer. Winter came on. Then came spring—an early spring.

The Little Men said, "Now go back to your home." They loaded him down with deer meat and berries. So he went.

Another man was going in that same direction. He met the man that had been lost so long, but he did not know him at first because the lost man was dressed in feathers and carried a large load. The other man spoke to him. So he was found, the man who had been lost so long ago.

This is the story of the man who was captured by the Little Men long ago.

The Dead Brought Back from the Other World

A man had a wife whom he loved very much. One day she tripped and fell into the fire. She was burned so bad she died.

The man was very sad. But he thought he saw her ghost go up into the sky. He went behind the house and found her trail. He followed it and reached the sky.

He saw her walk along the Milky Way. Following her, he could only catch up at night when she stopped to rest along the long, long trail. In this manner, catching up with her at night and losing her by day, he finally came to the Other World.

In the Other World all the dead were dancing and having a fine time. The husband watched them for a long while, then asked the Fire Tender if he might get his wife back.

"No, that is not possible," said the Fire Tender.

After awhile, the man fell asleep. It was daytime when he woke and all the dead were asleep. They lay like patches of soft white ashes on the ground.

The Fire Tender gave the husband a poker.

"If you poke the sleeping ghosts, the one that gets up as you do and sneezes will be your wife."

The sad man thus found his wife, picked her up and started home with her. At first she weighed nothing, but she became

35

heavier as he neared the earth and their house. Before he got there, he had to set down his burden and the ghost ran back to the Other World.

He followed her again and the next time got even closer to his door with her. But when he was forced to set her down once more because she weighed so much, she ran back again.

For the third time he returned to the Land of the Dead, but he was told that he could not try again.

"Go home," the Fire Tender said, "and in a short time you will be allowed to come and live with your wife."

The husband returned home and went to sleep. He died, and as a ghost returned to the Other World for good.

This story may remind you of the Greek myth, "Orpheus and Eurydice." In that story, the God of the Underworld takes pity on Orpheus and permits Eurydice to follow her husband back into the world. Orpheus is advised not to look back at her, but in his deep love and longing for her he does. It is in that moment that Eurydice is lost to Orpheus forever.

He followed her along the Milky Way.

The Lost Travelers

A trail went up on the other side of a river to a place where there was a ford.*

On this side of the river, just below the ford, there was a house. People who came upriver had to cross the river at the ford to get to this side. They had to wade across the river.

But there was an evil man who lived in the house. He would leave his house, go to the riverbank, grab his hooked pole, and catch the traveler. Then he would drown the traveler. For many moons he had drowned all travelers who passed his way. He piled them up along the riverbank.

One day a traveler named Urutsmaxig came along the trail. He was on his way to buy a wife. He watched carefully as he went along the trail, for he had heard that whoever waded across at the ford was caught and drowned. He saw the house across the river just as the trail turned down toward the river. The door was open and Urutsmaxig began to wonder what he should do. He waded halfway across the river when he felt his leg hooked.

The evil man with the hooked pole had caught him and tried to trip him, but the traveler struggled on and reached the other

*A ford is a shallow part of a body of water that can be crossed by wading.

Urutsmaxig overcomes evil.

37

side. He grabbed the hooked pole from the man and broke it into many pieces which he then threw into the river.

The evil one stood. He was surprised that anyone would seize his pole and break it. Urutsmaxig then lifted the evil one up and threw him into the river, too.

Then, finally, Urutsmaxig killed the evil one by drowning him. Urutsmaxig traveled on, always winning over evil.

Coyote Turns the People to Stone

Every day the people went out hunting deer. One day when they were hunting, Coyote saw them. He was far away on a mountain. He thought he would keep them from killing deer. He saw that they had their arrows on the bow strings. They were ready to shoot. Coyote didn't want any more deer killed.

"Pa-a-a-a-a!" he shouted. "Where are you going?"

The people turned to look at him. They turned to stone. They still stand there, where they stood. And that is all.

Coyote turns the people to stone.

Coyote and the Devil

A long time ago an evil being went around in the world eating people. He came to this country and came upriver.* The people heard of him, heard that a "Devil" who ate people was coming. They ran to live in the mountains.

Coyote asked them, "What are you afraid of? What is this *devil* you talk about? I am a devil, too. Perhaps we shall eat of each other. We will taste of each other."

Coyote got pitch from a tree in the forest and mixed it with earth and plants. He spread it thickly over his breast and his belly so that the evil one would taste that. He sat down by the fire to wait for the other to come. Badger sat hidden far away from the fire.

"Tatcididi kup kup kup!" was the sound they both heard. The evil one was coming down the trail.

"Now he is coming," said Coyote. "Don't worry. When I

---

*This refers to the Klamath River.

Coyote and the Devil

39

taste him, I will cut out his heart. Then I will come out of the house. You then run and open up the coals in the fire. I will jump on the roof and throw his heart in the fire. Then you must quickly cover it up with the coals!"

"*Tatcididi kup kup kup!*" they heard again.

"*Tatcididi kup kup kup!*" answered Coyote.

The devil was surprised to hear his own words spoken.

"Nowhere else have they said that to me before," he said.

"*He!*" said Coyote when he saw him. "I am hungry, for there are no people here to eat!"

"*Ho!*" said the devil. "I am hungry, too."

"Then let us eat each other," Coyote said.

"All right!" said the devil.

"You eat me first," said Coyote. He started up the fire and then opened his shirt. "Cut with this knife, right here, on the breast," he said as he pointed to the pitch-covered place.

"All right!" said the devil. And he cut a slice off Coyote's breast. He roasted it.

"Ah, you taste bitter."

"Yes," said Coyote. "It is because people have been talking about me."

The devil could hardly eat it; however, he ate until it was all gone.

"I'll taste you now," said Coyote.

"All right," said the devil. He uncovered his chest and Coyote took the knife and cut inside deeply. He cut in towards the heart and lungs and down to the bone.

"*A-a-a-a-a!*" said the devil. "A little higher. You cut too deep."

But Coyote kept on cutting close to the bone, and when he came to the end of the breastbone, he cut in deeper. He cut out the heart and lungs. He ran with them around the house and around and around, for the devil chased him. The devil came after Coyote.

Then Badger jumped out from his hiding place and opened the coals in the fire. Coyote jumped on the roof and threw the heart and lungs through the smoke-hole into the fire. Badger quickly covered them with hot coals. The heart opened and burst and the devil fell dead. People heard the sound of it bursting all over the world. That is how Coyote killed that devil.

TRICKSTERS

Coyote and Eagle

One day walking along the river carrying salmon, Coyote stopped to rest. On the other side of the river Eagle was perched high up in a tree.

"I wish Coyote would sleep soundly," thought Eagle.

And Coyote slept soundly.

Eagle flew down and took away all Coyote's salmon.

Eagle said, "Wake up! Get up!"

Coyote woke up. He turned over to eat and bit a stone. "Ouch!" said he, rubbing his mouth with his foot.

Coyote looked for his bundle of salmon, but found only the stick he carried it with. Then he looked up and saw Eagle across the river. Eagle was eating from Coyote's bundle of salmon.

"Divide it with me," Coyote begged Eagle, but Eagle ate it all.

So Coyote shot at him, but he did not hit him—Eagle was too far off.

Eagle flew down and took away all Coyote's salmon.

41

Coyote and the Rogue River People

Whenever the Rogue River people gambled they won everything, including all the other people with whom they played because they wagered persons, too.

An old woman lived in a house with her many children. Below, farther down the river, lived two other women.

Coyote came to where the old woman lived. She was his aunt. He came without any bed, but with him he carried his gambling sticks. She gave him some supper.

"Where are you going with your sticks?" she said.

"I am going to gamble," said Coyote.

"You are a clever one. Where is your wager?" said the old woman.

He took some beads out of his sack.

"You always want to do something," she said, and broke up his gambling sticks. She threw them into the fire.

Coyote saved one of the sticks.

The old woman made his bed for him.

"You can not strike me with anything," she said. She meant to give him some help in dodging sticks thrown at him. She put her rattles on her wrists, and she rattled them. She placed a basket of water nearby.

"If something should happen to me, sprinkle me with water and I shall come to life again," she said.

Then she gave him some dust that would help him win.

"Sprinkle me with water and I shall come to life again."

42

"Sit across from me," she said. Then she sang. "I am going to dance in this direction. You thought I was going that way. The Rogue River people will try to fool you, too."

So Coyote threw a stick at her and hit her. For a minute he forgot what to do to bring her to life again. Then he remembered and sprinkled her with the water in the basket. She breathed and sat up.

"Now you do the same," she said.

So Coyote did just as she had done. He sang her song and pretended to dance in one direction.

"Dodge about in every direction," the old woman instructed him.

"Look out!" she said, and she threw a stick in his direction, but he jumped up straight and escaped.

"You take this," she said. "Downriver are two fine women. You can wager them." She gave him special gambling sticks.

So Coyote went on. He went in a canoe and took many shell beads and blankets.

The two women downriver saw him and said, "See! A Chief is coming!"

Coyote married the two women and they all went on down the river.

They arrived at the place where people were gambling. He said to his wives, "Do not tell who I am. I will talk the Klamath language."

"What did you come for?" the people asked.

"I came to gamble," said Coyote.

"What have you to wager?" said the people.

"I have bead-money," said Coyote.

"No, that will not do," replied the Rogue River people. "We wager differently; we wager people."

Coyote said, "We do not wager people. I will wager bead-money."

"No," they said.

"I will even measure three fathoms of beads for you, four fathoms if you win," said Coyote.

"No!" said the Rogue River people. "We wager persons."

"All right," said Coyote. "I will wager myself and my two wives. Where are your gambling sticks?" asked Coyote.

"Where are yours?" they said. Coyote showed them.

Coyote had a little bird hidden in his hair behind his ear.

"We will throw at you first," the people said.

"All right," said Coyote, and he began to sing.

"They are going to pretend," said the little bird to Coyote, "so watch carefully."

The Rogue River people threw the sticks to knock over Coyote but he jumped straight up and so they missed.

"Now it is my turn," Coyote told them.

The bird said to Coyote, "Throw on that side. They will turn in that direction."

Coyote threw and knocked them down.

"Aha!" laughed Coyote, and so he won. He kept on knocking them down. In five days he won back all his own people from the Rogue River people.

Then the Rogue River people decided to play tricks on him. They wanted to win again. But Coyote knew all.

"Let us climb for eagles," they said. "There are some over there."

"All right," said Coyote. So they all ran over and came to a tree. Coyote climbed up. As he climbed, the tree stretched high up to the sky and became ice. It was so slippery Coyote could not climb down.

"We will throw at you first," the people said.

He threw down the young eagles.

"I don't know how I shall get down," he thought. He thought some more, and then he took some moss and floated down on that. He ran back and came to the place where he had gambled. So, again he won.

The Rogue River people were unhappy. They still wanted to win.

"Let us go and fish in that lake," they said.

"All right," said Coyote.

So they all went to the lake. There was a rattlesnake in there. Coyote took his spear and fished the snake out. Everyone ran away. Then he killed it. It really was a Rogue River person. Coyote then ran back to the gambling place. Again, he had won.

The Rogue River people still wanted to win because they always had won.

"Let us dive for dead salmon," they said.

"All right," said Coyote again, but he was getting tired of the games.

Little bird said to Coyote, "Take your arrow-flaker with you."

They went to the river and dove. Now Coyote was really tired and almost out of wind. He could not hold his breath any

"... he took some moss and floated down ..."

longer, but he got the salmon and rose to the top of the water with it. Then he hit his head against the ice for the bad people had caused the river to freeze. So with his arrow-flaker he made a hole in the ice and came out.

"Aha!" he said. "Here is your dead salmon to cook." So, again, he had won.

"Let us stop!" said the Rogue River people. "Instead, let us sweat."

"Take a flute with you," said the bird to Coyote.

Inside the sweat lodge the stones were red hot. Coyote went in first, but the heat was so great he would have died if he had not quickly dug a hole with the flute and got out alive. So, again, Coyote had won.

Now Coyote went off.

"Let us stop here," he said. "I will sleep here. I want to rest." So he slept. Soon it got dark. He woke.

"You must go back to my house," he told his wives. They went. Then he took three logs, three rotten logs, and he laid them side by side. He took a blanket and covered them so the bad people would think he was sleeping there. Then he went off a little way and leaned against a tree, watching.

Soon the Rogue River people came along. They had big stone knives. They struck and slashed the blanket-covered rotten logs. They knew now that Coyote had played a trick on them!

"You cannot catch or kill me!" Coyote laughed and ran away.

They followed him and were very close behind. Coyote jumped into some bushes.

"Let me become an old woman!" he said. "I must become an old woman!" And he became one.

"Hit him! That is the one!" yelled those people who chased him.

"Oh, oh, oh," the old woman sobbed. "The one you are following passed by me running very fast. I gave birth to your mother long ago. I am your grandmother. The other passed by running fast."

Coyote laughed to himself as they all ran on. Soon he came to a small creek. He jumped in, saying, "Let me become a salmon!" And so he did.

"That is the one! Spear it!" said the ones who followed.

"No! We will follow him," said one. "We will spear it coming back!"

46

"Ha!" laughed Coyote. "You will spear it coming back!" He jumped out.

Again they ran after him.

"Let me become a sedge!"* he said. He became one.

"Cut it, pull that up!" they said.

So Coyote jumped up and ran on. They followed him.

"Let me become a fog!" he said. And so he did, and there came rain and hail.

That is all.

---

*Sedge is any coarse, rush-like or flag-like herb growing in a wet place.

Further Reading

Dixon, R. B. "The Mythology of the Shasta-Achowami." *American Anthropologist*, Vol. VII, pp. 607-612.

——— *The Shasta.* Bulletin of the American Museum of Natural History. Vol XVII (July, 1907), Part V, pp. 381-498.

——— "Shasta Myths." *Journal of American Folklore*, Vol. XXIII (Jan.-March, 1910), No. 87. Boston: American Folklore Society.

Curtis, Edward S. *The North American Indian.* Vol. XIII. Landmarks in Anthropology Series. New York: Johnson Reprint Corp. 1976 (1924).

Heizer, R. F. and M. A. Whipple. *The California Indians.* Berkeley: University of California Press, 1951.

Holt, Catherine. "Shasta Ethnography." *Anthropological Records*, Vol. 3, No. 4, pp. 298-349, Berkeley: University of California Press, 1946.

Silver, Shirley. "Shastan Peoples." *Handbook of North American Indians.* Vol. 8, pp. 211-224, Washington, D.C.: Smithsonian Institution, 1978.

Swanton, J. R. *The Indian Tribes of North America.* Bulletin 145. Bureau of American Ethnology. Washington, D.C., 1950.